I0704479

A Tsunami of Sadness

By

Ivan Thompson

Table of Contents

Preface

I am a huge Dallas Cowboys football fan. Yesterday I watched an interview with Dak Prescott, the Cowboys' quarterback. In the interview, he shared the tragic news that his brother Jace had committed suicide.

When I woke up the next morning, I felt led to pray for Dak, his other brother, his family. As I was praying, I felt led to get up and write this book. This book is for anyone that struggles with depression, mood swings, recurring sadness, panic attacks, feelings of despair and helplessness, those who are distraught, those who have experienced so much pain that they have stopped feeling and shut down, and those who have had thoughts of taking their own life.

This book is also for people who have someone in their family circle, circle of friends, co-workers, perhaps even neighbors, workout buddies, etc., who seem to have either had a sudden shift in their behavior or have had lingering emotional problems like those I have described above. Your ability to notice any of these symptoms and ask the right questions may save someone's life.

In this book, I will share some of my own struggles with depression, panic attacks, and suicidal thoughts. My prayer is that someone will be helped.

A Tsunami of Sadness

The Google dictionary says that a tsunami is an arrival or occurrence of something in overwhelming quantities or amounts. The National Oceanic Atmospheric Administration (NOAA) says that "Tsunamis are giant waves…Tsunami waves may travel as fast as jet planes over deep waters…" (National Ocean Service, 2019)

There are many times in my life when suddenly, seemingly without warning, I have been swept away by a tsunami of sadness. A giant, overwhelming wave of despair or heaviness swoops in, knocks me off my feet, and sweeps me away. According to the NOAA, tsunamis are "caused by earthquakes or undersea volcanic eruptions." (National Ocean Service, 2019)

Many times in my experience with these tsunamis of sadness, I can't trace them back to a significant event, an earthquake in my life's events, or a disruption on the scale of a volcanic eruption. But a closer look at the definition helps me to see that maybe these gigantic waves of sadness are indeed connected to big disruptions, but the delay in the wave's arrival causes me not to see the connection:

"Tsunamis are giant waves caused by earthquakes or volcanic eruptions under the sea. Out in the depths of the ocean, tsunami waves do not dramatically increase in height. But as the waves travel inland, they build up to higher and higher heights as the depth of the ocean decreases." (National Ocean Service, 2019)

I can see how something traumatic like the loss of my kids in divorce produced waves that initially didn't "dramatically increase in height" but built "up to higher and higher heights over time." Similarly, I can see where perhaps the death of a friend, a huge disappointment, rejection, or any childhood trauma that had not been fully processed could shift under the surface of my emotions, like the shifting of the "tectonic plates" that causes earthquakes. (USGS, n.d.)

I can see how the "plates" of unresolved traumas could shift over and over in my life, causing emotional disruptions that are unnoticeable at first and then seem to arrive as a surprise wave of giant negative emotions. In my life, I can see how these plate shifts could be triggered by even the smallest things. As a divorced dad, it could be something like regret over not being able to make a birthday or anything that seems like rejection from my kids.

If you have ever seen footage of a tsunami, you know that when the wave arrives, it is most often too late to run. Everything in its path gets swept away. If I can learn what my triggers are (rejection, shame, the perception that I am failing in life, etc.) I can begin to prepare for the tsunami before it hits, even though I don't currently see any large emotional waves.

Knowing that I am triggered acts as its own early warning/tsunami detection system and gives me a head start as I run to seek high ground, safety from the unseen wave of emotions that I know is coming.

In practical terms, if I have experienced rejection from a significant person, if I have had a recent personal failure, I can schedule a meeting with my therapist, reach out to an accountability partner, email or call some friends, long before the wave shows up.

If I have been triggered, I know that my emotional plates have been shifted under the surface. The big waves are coming. I know they are coming, even if I don't immediately sense anything. Doing nothing is like standing on the beach and waiting to see the wave and then trying to outrun it. I will most certainly be swept away in a wave of negative emotions that could have devastating consequences.

Suicidal At Seven?

The first time I thought about killing myself, I was somewhere between seven and nine years old. I will be 56 this month (Sep 2020), but I still remember it vividly. It was late at night, and I walked into the kitchen. The street and traffic lights made what looked like a lion's mane on the window. On the counter of the kitchen sink, I saw a butcher knife, and all I remember thinking was that I should kill myself. I remember the incredible sadness associated with that house.

So many bad things happened in that house, so many terrible memories, some of my most traumatic. I believe it is why I cannot remember a lot of things from my childhood. I believe, for my own protection, that many of my childhood memories have been blocked out.

I know the question for the reader may be what happened to him? What happened is not the issue. Suffice it to say that the things that happened were terrible for me. Many people have experienced greater trauma and loss and have not had thoughts of suicide or lingering depression. In my own life experience, I have seen that people can have similar traumatic experiences, even in the same household, without producing the same kind of negative effects. I believe the reason for the different effects is due to differences in temperament and personality.

I am a very sensitive person. I guess I always have been. I believe this personality trait, combined with the terrible things that happened during my childhood and the influence of the demonic, brought me to the point of considering taking my own life in the third or fourth grade.

When I say demonic, I mean that as a child, I distinctly remember seeing black images, dark shadows flitting through the house. I remember one terrifying encounter with what I believe was a demonic entity. Though I had many terrible nightmares involving demons, I believe that many of these instances happened while I was awake and at home alone.

In Psalm 18, verse five, David says, "The sorrows of hell compassed me about: the snares of death prevented me." This Scripture captures the feeling that I am trying to express when I describe the depression that I have gone through. When I am depressed, it's as if "the sorrows of hell" have surrounded me and I feel trapped to the point where it seems that there is no escape. I have had those feelings off and on my entire life.

When I looked up the phrase "the sorrows of hell," I saw it three times in Scripture, 2 Sam 22:6, Psalm 18:5, and Psalm 116:3. It appears that David encountered this type of sadness on several occasions. That was encouraging to me. If one of God's greatest warriors experienced this kind of attack on more than one occasion, then I guess it's ok for me too.

I say attack because I believe that often it is a demonic attack—more on that in a moment. Yes, I do believe that there may be a genetic component to my experience that predisposes me to depression and panic attacks. My father struggled with severe depression and suicidal thoughts. I also know from digging into the family history on my father's side that there is some history of depression and mental illness. And, as I have described above, I believe that the effects of childhood trauma also contributed to my mental and emotional condition. However, there is a spiritual component that, if missed, could prove deadly.

The Bible in John 10:10 says that the devil comes "to steal, kill, and to destroy." That's his mission. That's his aim with everything he comes in contact with, including you and I. He wants to take us out. The devil knows that we are made in the likeness, the image of God. He knows how much God cares for us. And since he can't destroy or harm God, he attacks us. The good news, though, is that in that same verse, Jesus said, "I have come that they may have life and that they may have it more abundantly."

Make no mistake, Jesus' plan for your life is for you to live, to be happy, to overcome sorrow, to find a way out of what seems to be surrounding you. The devil is a liar, and the Bible calls him the father of lies. If you are looking at what he's showing you and listening to what he says, you will not see or hear a way out. Everything will be overwhelming, helpless. Your imagination at that moment is only being influenced by sorrow, in fact, the very sorrows of hell.

If you miss the fact that you are in a spiritual battle, some of the other helpful things that I will mention may not help. I have heard many people say, "I'm a very spiritual person." That's not really biblically correct. The Bible says that God is "the father of spirits." (Heb 12:9)

You are a spirit, you live in a body, and you possess a soul. You are a three-part being. To be effective in what could be a battle for your life, you have to realize that some of the help you need will be spiritual.

Following David's Example

I have always personified "the sorrows of hell." Specifically, I have always treated these "sorrows" as spirit beings. When David says he was "compassed about," and when I say I feel "surrounded," I mean it literally. It's as if a company, a band, a gang of demons has surrounded me. In the New International Version of the Bible, Psalm 18:5 reads, "The cords of the grave coiled around me; the snares of death confronted me."

I know that every time I experience depression, despair, or panic, it is not the result of a spiritual attack or the presence of demons, but the purpose of this segment of the book is to point out that it could be and what our response should be. I will address other ways that I deal with depression in later chapters.

I think David's example, his response to the sorrows of hell, is a good one to follow. The Bible portrays David as a worshipper as he wrote many of the psalms. According to one Bible scholar, "the biggest category of psalms" were "songs" and "melodies." The same scholar said that "The Hebrew word for psalm, mizmôr, means 'melody.'" (Kranz, 2014)

We also know that when the ark of the covenant was brought to Jerusalem that David, even though he was the king, worshipped so powerfully that he danced out of his clothes:

"The Ark Brought to Jerusalem
When those carrying the ark of the LORD
had advanced six paces, he sacrificed an
ox and a fattened calf. And
David, wearing a
linen ephod, danced with all his
might before the LORD, while he and all
the house of Israel brought up the ark of
the LORD with shouting and the sounding
of the ram's horn..." Berean Study Bible

If we tie what we know about David as a worshipper to what his response was when he experienced the "sorrows of hell," we get something that we can use when we experience similar feelings:

2Sa 22:4-7

I will **call on the LORD**, who is worthy to be **praised**: so shall I be saved from mine enemies. When the waves of death compassed me, the floods of ungodly men made me afraid; The sorrows of hell compassed me about; the snares of death prevented me; **In my distress I called upon the LORD**, and cried to my God: and he did hear my voice out of his temple, and my cry did enter into his ears.

Psa 18:1-6 [[To the chief Musician, A Psalm of David, the servant of the LORD, who spake unto the LORD the words of this **song** in the day that the LORD delivered him from the hand of all his enemies, and from the hand of Saul: And he said,]] I will love thee, O LORD, my strength. **The LORD is my rock, and my fortress, and my deliverer; my God, my strength, in whom I will trust; my buckler, and the horn of my salvation, and my high tower**. I will call upon the LORD, who is worthy to be praised: so shall I be saved from mine enemies. The sorrows of death compassed me, and the floods of ungodly men made me afraid. The sorrows of hell compassed me about: the snares of death prevented me. In my distress **I called upon the LORD**, and cried unto my God: he heard my voice out of his temple, and my cry came before him, even into his ears.

Psa 116:1-5 I love the LORD, because he hath heard my voice and my

supplications. Because he hath inclined his ear unto me, therefore **will I call upon him as long as I live**. The sorrows of death compassed me, and the pains of hell gat hold upon me: I found trouble and sorrow. **Then called I upon the name of the LORD; O LORD**, I beseech thee, deliver my soul. **Gracious is the LORD, and righteous; yea, our God is merciful**.

The Swirlies

I used to call the onset of serious episodes of depression "the swirlies." The image is that of water in a toilet as it is being flushed. It represented my emotions, just going further and further down. Another appropriate analogy would be a whirlpool in the ocean that sucks everything down near its path. When "the swirlies" started, I often felt helpless to keep my whole life from seemingly being sucked down in the swirl.

From David's example, we see that when he was in emotional "distress," he called upon the Lord, sang praise, offered gratitude to the Lord, sang out the Lord's positive attributes, and by faith, was reassured that the Lord heard him. David in 2 Sam 22:17-20 says:

"He sent from above, he took me; he **drew me out of many waters**; He delivered me from my strong enemy, and from them that hated me: for they were too strong for me. They prevented me in the day of my calamity: but the LORD was my stay. He brought me forth also into a large place: he delivered me, because he delighted in me.

David said that God responded from above and drew him "out of many waters." I can't find in Scripture where David was ever in danger of drowning. So perhaps David envisioned emotional distress similar to the way that I have, as overwhelming waters, or "the swirlies." When "the swirlies" showed up in David's life, he called upon God, worshipped God, was grateful to God, and God sent a mighty deliverance.

2 Chro 20:22 is another example of using praise to stop the enemy's attack: "As they began to sing and praise, the Lord set ambushes against the men of Ammon and Moab and Mount Seir who were invading Judah, and they were defeated."

I have seen these Scriptures. I have heard many sermons on the subject of praise as a weapon. I am a professional singer. I have sung in stadiums and arenas for national sporting events, sang on television, and in touring shows. I have written and recorded praise songs and sung on praise teams. However, when "the swirlies" hit, it is often the hardest thing in the world to combat them with praise. It is something that I still struggle with.

I can testify, though, that every time I can make myself respond the way David did to his "distress" and "many waters," that it ALWAYS works. Sometimes if I can just say "JESUS," it works! Perhaps you struggle with your spiritual response too. Keep working at it. God loves you and is ready to help when you call on Him and worship Him in faith.

Isolation, Secrecy, Shame, and Suffering

Isolation, Secrecy, Shame, and Suffering are four things that should never be mixed together. Based on my journey towards better mental health, I can tell you definitively that the worst thing that you can do is try to battle mental illness, depression, or prolonged sadness alone. It is not a Christian virtue to suffer in solitude. If you have ever watched wrestling, the worst place to be is alone in the corner of the ring, where you can't tag your partner.

I know that sometimes there are things that we have done that cause us to want to retreat into isolation. Shame is a powerful force that will pull you into a dark place away from help. Shame's close companion is secrecy. Shame convinces you that secrecy is the best way to protect yourself when secrecy is, in fact, another form of isolation.

I have found that I am more spiritually, emotionally, and mentally healthy when I open up to people. I am healthier when I have an outlet for my secrets and actions that have caused me to feel shame. I have participated in Christian and non-Christian 12 Step groups, men's groups, accountability groups, and all were helpful.

Shame says that sharing the things you are ashamed of will only bring deeper levels of shame. There are times when I have shared things with immature people and even unseasoned leaders in the body of Christ that caused me to experience more pain and shame. But my testimony is, despite a few failed and unfortunate attempts, there is tremendous liberty in escaping the bondage of secrets and dispelling shame. The freedom you experience as you offload shameful secrets is far greater than the benefit gained by "protecting yourself" in isolation.

The truth is that I was a slave to shame and secrets. I thought I had them under control. But in reality, I was on a chain and could only go so far, and every now and then, they'd surface to torment me. No, everyone is not a "safe" person to tell your secrets to. But God will provide a way of escape from the suffering you are experiencing as it relates to shame and secrets. The way of escape will always be found in the company of others.

A New Circle

In the Scriptures quoted, David described himself as being encircled by the sorrows of hell and the snares of death. On my mental health journey, I had to break out of that circle and establish a new circle.

My new circle is fluid but usually contains healthy friendships (that I have built and sustained over the years), accountability partners, a therapist, pastors, activity partners, family members, and the Holy Spirit.

I meet a lot of people. In my military career, I met people by while being assigned at the same base, working in the same office. I also went to a military Academy and served with several of my Academy classmates at the different places where I was stationed. Our common military background gave us a common bond and, for me, was at least one source of friends.

Because the military relocated me from base to base, I have also made friends around the country at the different churches where I have been stationed. My church friends tend to be a little closer because our friendship encompassed a spiritual aspect and often accountability on a level more personal than with my military friends.

I have been the best man at some of these friends' weddings. I am the godfather of another friend's kids. I tend to be able to talk about more serious and troubling concerns and spiritual matters with these friends.

Activity partners. I read in another book years ago that everyone in my circle of friends won't be a confidant, close personal friend, or best friend material. Some of my friends are friends that I just watch football with, workout with, or friends at work. I typically don't spend time with my "work friends" outside the workplace. The point is the more friendly faces you have in your circle, the more people you can have healthy interactions with.

I don't currently have a spouse, but of course, your spouse or significant other should be near the top of the list of people you confide in. As a person who has experienced divorce, I also know that some of the problems you are having could involve that spouse. If so, marriage counselors, pastors, and therapists are a good outlet so that you don't bottle up your feelings.

Family members. Just like you can talk about different things with different friends, I know which family members I can talk to when I'm battling depression or despair. I have one family member that I call my "9-1-1." If I'm in crisis, she would be the first person that I would call.

Every relationship, friendship has to be maintained. The more you invest in the relationship, the more that you will be able to withdraw from those investments when you need them. It's unreasonable to expect a high level of commitment or support from relationships and friendships that you haven't invested in. The notion that you don't need anyone is just a flat-out lie. Do the work to build mutually supportive relationships.

The Holy Spirit. Having an intimate relationship with the Holy Spirit is essential as a Christian and to your mental health. There are so many times when the Holy Spirit has led me out of mental health problems by leading me to journal my feelings, schedule therapy appointments I was delaying, apologize, write letters to loved ones, call a friend or accountability partner, repent, pray, worship, etc. The Holy Spirit has led me to do whatever was needed at the moment to get me unstuck.

"Search me, God, and know my heart; test me and know my anxious thoughts. See if there is any offensive way in me, and lead me in the way everlasting."

Psalm 139:23-24 (NIV)

"I, the LORD, search the heart, I test the mind, Even to give every man according to his ways, According to the fruit of his doings."

Jer 17:10 (NKJV)

"O LORD, You have searched me and known me. You know when I sit and when I rise; You understand my thoughts from afar. You search out my path and my lying down; You are aware of all my ways."

Psalm 139:1-3 (BSB)

God knows our thoughts, our proclivities, our tendencies, and all the ways we tend to get into mental and emotional crises. Through the Holy Spirit, the Helper, God can communicate things directly in our hearts and conscious mind that will help.

Little Boy Go to Sleep

I remember when my son was three or four years old that he just did not want to go to bed. I'd get him in bed, and so often, he'd say he "forgot" to brush his teeth or that he had to go to the bathroom. He'd do anything to stay up just a little longer. Even when he was in bed, I could see those steely green-grey eyes peeking out at me; he just wouldn't go to sleep! He must have thought that he would be missing something.

I'm 55, and I'm the same way. I have learned that a lot of times, I am off track emotionally because I am tired. I used to think that taking naps during the day was for "old people." It wasn't until I was around 50 that I finally made it ok for me to take a nap during the day or to make a regular bedtime a priority.

Things tend to upset me more easily when I'm very tired. I'm a "type-A" personality, and I can lock into a goal for hours a day, day after day. I can lock myself away with something, like writing this book, and try to write the whole thing in a day. I can focus on a yard project for hours, delaying water and shade breaks—not a good thing in Phoenix, Arizona. I'm like the little boy who thinks that he will miss something if he takes a nap or goes to bed early.

I've already said that we are spirits that live in a body and possess a soul. In gaining relief from depression, I must address the spiritual and emotional/mental aspects of my health, but I must also take care of my body. Rest is a big part of that. I had to learn that. I had to unlearn that resting was lazy.

In addition to rest, I also have to have healthy exercise and eating habits! I have a fitness page (IG, FB, YouTube, Twitter) and a fitness book on Amazon, where I talk more about fitness. Bottom line: I know that if I am exercising regularly, eating right, and getting plenty of rest, I am less susceptible to bouts of depression and despair.

Mental Health and the Church

I have had some dramatic breakthroughs that came as a direct result of having hands laid on me in prayer. I used to have debilitating panic attacks that started, as best as I can recall, shortly after my divorce. Being alone somehow triggered panic attacks in which I would scream, cry, yell, or collapse on the floor in fear or despair. I almost could not stand to be alone.

I experienced healing and relief from these type attacks for several years after one dramatic prayer for depression at the altar. Years later, when these attacks tried to make a resurgence, I listened to a Word of Faith sermon on a CD that again prevented the panic attacks for an extended period of time.

Despite my testimony above, however, I have had great struggles with the Church and their response to my mental health issues. I use church with a capital "C" because it has been my experience at more than one church. My worst experiences have come at churches where the "Word of God" and "faith" have been emphasized the most.

Even the healing I referred to above happened at a church where I felt mental illness was equated with a lack of spiritual strength or lack of faith. Though I have learned the most from Word of Faith teachers and pastors, and the content of most of my books has been heavily influenced by them, many times, their views on treatment for mental health problems haven't been that healthy.

No credible Word of Faith pastor or teacher would ever tell someone not to go to the doctor if they were experiencing pain in their body. But these same leaders often applied a different standard for someone experiencing sickness in their brain or emotions.

Somehow then a "faith" or Scriptural solution seemed to be the only "godly" or Christian solution. If a person was experiencing arthritis or "migraines," for example, they might be encouraged to come to the altar for prayer, but they would not be discouraged from taking pain medication or seeing their doctor.

Many times, I was made to feel as if my faith wasn't big enough or that I was not spiritual enough because I was seeing a therapist. This negative stigma often caused me to second-guess going to therapy and just try to stand in faith. Even if therapy was reluctantly considered as an option by my pastors, it was only ok if it was a "Christian" therapist.

Though I understand the caution about what kind of therapist you should have, I have had great success with therapists, Christian and non-Christian. One of my greatest therapists was an atheist, biker-chic. God used this woman and my willingness to open up to achieve significant breakthroughs related to clearing out unforgiveness in my heart.

My point in this chapter is to point out that you may need help in more than one area. You may need spiritual help, therapy, support groups, friends, confidants, medication, and it's ok. Do whatever you need to do to get healthy and to stay healthy. Just as God can use doctors and the science that they rely on, I believe He can use psychologists even if some of the underlying tenets of their science don't always seem to follow Scripture.

How will you know you are getting better? The same way you would know if you were getting better with some other type of illness or pain, the symptoms will lessen in intensity, duration, frequency, etc. Get help. Keep searching for help until your mental health improves.

Mental Health and the Air Force

I had a Top Secret clearance in the military. It was a requirement for my job. My mental health, however, was a consideration for keeping the clearance. Though we had mental health clinics in the Air Force, going to the clinic, going to see a psychologist was seen as something that could cost you your security clearance. It's understandable why the Air Force wouldn't want mentally unstable people possessing access to classified data. However, tying a person's mental health to their ability to keep their clearance had the side effect of causing people to hide their problems vs. seek help. That was twenty years ago. The Air Force has since changed its view and has actively sought to reduce the stigma of going to the mental health clinic.

I remember back then that I would pay for my therapy sessions with a private psychologist so that I could hide them from the Air Force. I would later have to admit these visits on my periodic recertifications for my clearance but going to the mental health clinic was something that immediately went into your military medical records.

I was able to do this until 2000. In 2000, I separated from my wife in Hampton, Virginia. She and four of my five kids moved to Arizona while I was sent to the Pentagon. It caused me to experience a great deal of depression. Perhaps the worst in my life. I remember having one too many thoughts of throwing myself in front of a subway train. It caused me to go to the mental health clinic and not care about the consequences. My military psychologist helped me to develop coping strategies related to losing my kids.

Once as a military supervisor, a person in one of my work centers put a suicide note on his desk. Someone found the note, and we were able to get the person some help. In another incident, I remember asking a young airman if he was thinking of harming himself based on his reaction to an unscheduled deployment. He said yes, and I was able to get him connected to the military chaplain for help.

I'd gone through suicide prevention training that taught us to ask if a person was considering harming themselves, and if so, where, when, how (the plan), and to call for help. I went through a civilian version of that training years later in Arizona. It helped me ask a similar question of someone who I didn't know well. Based on his reaction, I was able to call the police and found out that here in our area, they do "wellness checks." They went and checked on the person to ensure that he was ok.

You may not be in the military, but perhaps your employer has similar training. If so, I recommend it; you may be able to help save someone's life. At the very least, you could be the reason someone finally decides to get some help.

Be Supportive

Recently I was watching the NBA playoffs, and I saw a segment featuring six-time All-Star Paul George of the Los Angeles Clippers. He was sharing how being sequestered away in the NBA "Bubble" had caused him to suffer depression. For him, these feelings were unanticipated. He then went on to share how he got some counseling and felt better. You would think that someone who has battled depression, panic attacks, and suicidal thoughts as much as I have would have had sympathy for him. I didn't at first.

My first thought was, "you're a multi-millionaire, what do you have to be depressed about?" I then went on to think about how military members are sent on deployments and remote assignments and are separated from their families for months, even up to a year at a time. Then the Holy Spirit reminded me of Deion Sanders, a Hall of Fame Football player who played for the Falcons, Niners, Cowboys, Redskins, and Ravens.

Years ago, I watched Deion Sanders' testimony in which he shared that all the fame of being known as "Prime-Time" and winning multiple Super Bowls weren't enough to make him happy. He said he won a second Super Bowl, and shortly after, he was depressed. He later went on to attempt suicide.

I had no right to look at what Paul George had materially and say that he had less of a right than I did to experience depression, especially during COVID-19. I had to repent. A similar thing happened when Skip Bayless, co-host of Fox Sports' "Undisputed," criticized Dak Prescott for going public with his battle with depression:

> "Bayless criticized Dallas Cowboys quarterback Dak Prescott for revealing on an upcoming episode of "In Depth with Graham Bensinger" that he dealt with depression and began experiencing anxiety in the early stages of the coronavirus shutdown. Then in mid-April his older brother, Jace, died by suicide, which brought a new wave of emotions. Bayless said that while he has sympathy for those with clinical depression, he has no sympathy for Prescott because as quarterback of "America's team" he's supposed to be a leader of men.

> "I have deep compassion for clinical depression, but when it comes to the quarterback of an NFL team, you [Shannon Sharpe] know this better than I do, it's the ultimate leadership position in sports, am I right about that?"

Bayless said on "Undisputed". "You are commanding an entire franchise… And they're all looking to you to be their CEO, to be in charge of the football team.

"Because of all that, I don't have sympathy for him going public with, 'I got depressed,' 'I suffered depression early in COVID to the point that I couldn't even go work out.' Look, he's the quarterback of America's team …

"The sport that you play, it is dog eat dog. It is no compassion, no quarter given on the football field. If you reveal publicly any little weakness, it can affect your team's ability to believe in you in the toughest spots and it can definitely encourage others on the other side to come after you."

Do not listen to Skip Bayless.

A leader of men does what Prescott did. Being vulnerable does not make Prescott less of a leader. For locker rooms that constantly preach "family," it could bring his teammates closer and lead to a new level of respect, and perhaps to some of them revealing their own bouts with depression, whether brief or ongoing.

You know, being human. Showing love and support to one another, like families do.

For far too long, men in particular have suffered through mental illness in silence because of toxic attitudes like Bayless's, and this is especially acute in the Black community where for too long mental health discussions have been stigmatized or met with a recommendation to "pray more" in lieu of getting help from a professional, which results in Black Americans seeking mental health about half as often as others (lack of health insurance contributes as well)." (Young, 2020)

Skip Bayless' comments and my thoughts couldn't have had any worse timing. This is National Suicide Prevention Week. I know as well as anyone that prolonged sadness and despair can lead to suicide. I was a person who, as a child, was in the same house as someone who attempted suicide. I know better than to take the topic of depression and prolonged sadness lightly. I also had a high school classmate that committed suicide in mid-life.

When you read the statistics for African American men, there is no question that we should be providing even greater support for these men when they take the brave step of coming forward and asking for help. It should be applauded, not ridiculed. The support and encouragement that we provide to those in our circle of influence could save someone's life.

Thank you Paul George, Dak Prescott, Deion Sanders, and the many other brave men and women in various fields for being honest about your mental health struggles!

Suicide Hotline

National Suicide Prevention Lifeline

Available **24 hours**. Languages: English, Spanish.

800-273-8255

Helpful Links:

https://suicidepreventionlifeline.org/

National Institute on Minority Health and Health Disparities (NIMHD) http://www.nimhd.nih.gov

National Institute of Mental Health, http://www.nimh.nih.gov

Substance Abuse and Mental Health Services Administration, http://www.samhsa.gov

National Alliance on Mental Illness, http://www.nami.org

Mental Health America, http://www.mentalhealthamerica.net/african-american-mental-health

Other Books By the Author:

Amazon
https://bit.ly/ivantheauthor

Audible
https://bit.ly/IvanThompson

*25 Essential Bible Verses for Christian Business Leaders
25 Bible Verses for Dads
Finding Next A Book of Divine Seasons
Financial Testimonies Stories of God's Grace and Provision
First Responders a Revelation of the Love of Jesus
Lifesaving The Importance of Hearing the Voice of God
Fit @ 50
Increasing Your Skills and Abilities in Any Area
Letters to Build a Young Man's Confidence
No Grandma It's an e-book
The Air Force's Black Ceiling
The Air Force's Black Pilot Training Experience
The Bible Promises of Healing 16 Letters for Mom
The Making of a Great America Where the Founding Fathers and the Church Fell Short
The Making of a Great America Uprooting the Spirit of Racism
The Making of a Great America Made in the Image of Trump

*You Should Detours and Distractions to Divine Destiny
*Also available in Spanish (print and audiobook)

Bibliograhphy

Kranz, J. (2014, Jun 11). *The 8 Types of Psalms in the Bible.* Retrieved from https://overviewbible.com/: https://overviewbible.com/kinds-of-psalms/

National Ocean Service. (2019, November 13). Retrieved from What is a tsunami?: https://oceanservice.noaa.gov/facts/tsunami.html

USGS. (n.d.). *What is an earthquake and what causes them to happen?* Retrieved from USGS.gov: https://www.usgs.gov/faqs/what-earthquake-and-what-causes-them-happen?qt-news_science_products=0#qt-news_science_products

Young, S. M. (2020, Sep 10). *Skip Bayless has no right to criticize Dak Prescott's honesty about mental health.* Retrieved from Yahoo Sports: https://sports.yahoo.com/skip-bayless-dak-prescott-mental-health-215536925.html?soc_src=community&soc_trk=ma

www.ingramcontent.com/pod-product-compliance
Lightning Source LLC
Chambersburg PA
CBHW051134250726

48655CB00007B/3059